THE WEALTH BUILDER'S BLUEPRINT

Mastering the 7 Steps to Financial Prosperity"

BY

Roberta W-. Blanton

TABLE OF CONTENTS

ABOUT THE BOOK

"Mastering Wealth: 7 Steps to Financial Success" is your reliable guide to prosperity in a world where achieving financial success is both a desired objective and a difficult undertaking. With the guidance of this thorough and entertaining book, you will be able to successfully negotiate the challenging world of wealth creation and secure a better future.

Unlock the 7 Key Steps to Financial Success:

1. The Wealth Mindset

Your financial path begins with an understanding of the psychology of wealth. Discover how to overcome limiting beliefs, develop a good money attitude, and master goal-setting and visualisation to influence your financial reality.

2. Financial Education

The foundation of sound financial management is sound financial literacy. This chapter, which embraces both formal and self-learning, demystifies the significance of financial education. It emphasises the need of ongoing education while laying the foundation for wise personal financial management.

3. Savings and Budgeting

Learn the techniques for developing a sensible budget that will enable you to take charge of your money. Discover how to reduce wasteful spending and discover how to automate your savings as you explore the mysteries of compound interest.

4. Prudent Investing

Explore a variety of investment vehicles, such as stocks, bonds, real estate, and more, and learn about risk management and diversification to help demystify the world of investing. Recognise the distinction between investing for the long term and short term, and create a solid investment plan.

5. Income Generation and Entrepreneurship

Investigate the world of entrepreneurship and discover how to use your interests and abilities to generate many sources of income. Strike a balance between work security and entrepreneurship to create the conditions for financial wealth.

6. Handling Debt

Develop efficient debt repayment plans, become an expert at identifying good debt from bad debt, and become skilled at negotiating reduced interest rates. Take tackle the mental effects of debt and financial strain head-on.

7. Investing in Real Estate to Build Wealth

Explore the exciting field of real estate investing. This chapter offers the information you need, whether you're thinking about real estate investment trusts (REITs), rental properties, property flipping, or managing and maintaining your real estate portfolio.

Why "Mastering Wealth" is a Must-Read:

This book is a thorough guide to help you grasp and become an expert in the art of wealth-building, not just a collection of financial tips. Whatever your financial situation right now, "Mastering Wealth" gives you the knowledge and resources you need to set out on the path to financial success.

Easily readable, captivating, and perceptive, this book is meant to serve as a useful tool for novice and seasoned investors alike. Whether your objective is to create a legacy of prosperity, attain financial independence, or secure a happy retirement, it enables you to realise your full financial potential.

Discover the Power of Financial Mastery:

As you read "Mastering Wealth: 7 Steps to Financial Success," you'll learn more about how to handle the challenges associated with financial success. This book is your go-to resource for helpful advice, practical tactics, and real-world examples as you progress towards financial mastery.

"Mastering Wealth" is your manual for turning your financial aspirations into reality, whether your goals are to leave a lasting legacy, build a solid financial future, or become financially independent to follow your passions. It's time to go out on your financial success path, and this book is your reliable road map.

Chapter 1: The Wealth Mindset

It's common knowledge in the field of wealth building that the journey starts inside. The most important resource of all must be developed before one can accumulate wealth, investments, and possessions: a wealth mindset. The creation of wealth is closely related to how we think about and view money; it is not only about sound financial judgment or clever investment choices. We will explore the complex network of ideas, preconceptions, and attitudes that underpin your financial future in this chapter.

Gaining insight into the psychology of riches is akin to discovering a hidden treasure trove of possibilities. It's about realizing that in your pursuit of riches, your thinking may be either a strong ally or a dangerous enemy. You may have heard tales of those who seem to draw wealth with ease, while others, despite their greatest efforts, struggle. The strength of one's mentality is sometimes blamed for this phenomenon.

We will examine the idea of a positive money attitude as a starting point for our path toward a wealth mindset. A positive money mindset involves adopting a set of attitudes and beliefs that enable you to take charge of your financial future. It goes beyond simply thinking optimistically. We'll explore the components of this way of thinking, from having fearlessness while making financial decisions to being grateful for what you already have.

Limiting thoughts is one of the biggest obstacles to wealth building. These ideas are the subdued, enduring whispers that nag at us, reminding us that we lack the skills or abilities necessary to succeed financially. One of the most important steps in turning yourself into a money generator is realizing and conquering these limiting ideas. We'll look at techniques for identifying, disputing, and finally defeating these ideas.

We will also look at the transforming potential of goal-setting and visualization in this chapter. The route plan for your financial journey is provided by your goals, and the means of transportation to get there is visualization. These instruments, when used wisely, can assist you in bringing your dreams to pass. We'll talk about how to make a clear mental image of your ideal financial future and how to develop meaningful financial goals.

Your mentality is where your riches path starts. By the time you finish reading this chapter, you will know how ideas, attitudes, and goals interact to determine how your finances turn out. With the knowledge and resources you'll need to develop a wealth mindset, you'll be ready for the step-by-step instructions on achieving financial success that are provided in the upcoming chapters.

Greetings and welcome to the process of realizing your financial potential. We are going to take a revolutionary look at the wealth mindset on the pages that follow. This is the starting point, the basis on which financial fantasies come true and fortunes are made.

Think of your financial attitude as the compass that guides your decisions, activities, and eventually the process of accumulating money. We'll go deep into the nuances of your connection with money in this chapter, and we'll talk about how your perspective can make or break your financial success.

Our guiding concept for this chapter is the wealth mindset, a multifaceted gem made up of several crucial elements. We'll go through four important areas:

1.   Understanding the Psychology of Wealth: In this section, the intricacies of human psychology about money will be dissected. We'll explore the ingrained convictions, driving forces, and anxieties that frequently shape our financial choices. Gaining insight into the psychological foundations of wealth will enable you to make deliberate decisions free from the imperceptible barriers that may impede your advancement.

2.   Developing a Positive Money attitude: Having a positive money attitude entails more than just being upbeat about your future finances. It is a comprehensive strategy for improving your financial well-being that begins with gratitude, cultivates plenty, and gives you confidence in your financial judgment. We will look at how to develop a mindset that can be your financial launching pad.

3.   Recognising Limiting Beliefs and Overcoming Them: One of the most important steps on your path to financial success is realizing and facing your limiting beliefs. Without you even realizing it, these deeply rooted mental habits have the potential to undermine your success. You may start to break down the obstacles that have been preventing you from moving forward and make room for a wealth-oriented mindset by learning to recognize and confront them.

4.   The Influence of Visualisation and Goal-Setting: Your goals serve as your compass amid the wide ocean of financial options. They provide you with focus, inspiration, and a clear route to achieving your financial goals. Establishing worthwhile and attainable financial objectives can provide you with direction and a clear path forward. We'll also talk about the practice of visualization, which uses the mind's amazing potential to help you bring your dreams to life.

Let's now set out on this life-changing adventure through the wealth mindset, equipping you with the skills and information necessary to build enduring financial prosperity. The first thing you should do is learn about the psychology of riches.

Chapter 2: Financial Education

Your best ally in the quest for riches and financial success is education. Entering Chapter 2, "Financial Education," we take a deep dive into your financial empowerment and knowledge. Here, we delve into the complex network of ideas and precepts that form the basis of your knowledge of money, prosperity, and financial security.

We will explore the essential elements of financial literacy in this chapter, understanding that these ideas form the cornerstone of your financial destiny. As we go along, you'll see how important financial literacy is to your quest for success and financial freedom.

We start our investigation with a basic fact: financial knowledge matters. In the contemporary world, financial literacy is a necessity, not a luxury. It's the vocabulary of finance, the aptitude for understanding financial ideas, and the ability to make wise financial decisions. We will explore financial literacy's importance and how it might enable you to take charge of your financial future.

There are two main types of education: self-education and formal education. We shall examine the differences and benefits of each. Formal education offers structured knowledge and is typically obtained through schools, courses, and professional training. On the other side, self-education gives you the freedom to learn and explore at your own pace. When combined, these two methods produce a well-rounded education that gives you the skills you need to successfully negotiate the challenging world of finance.

Our next goal is to lay a solid foundation in personal finance. This means being aware of the basic ideas behind personal finance management, such as setting up a budget, saving money, investing, and handling debt. The basis of your financial future is your personal finance system. You will be equipped to make informed decisions that advance your financial goals by carefully considering this issue.

However, once you've established your foundation, learning never stops. That's just the start of it. The last continuous theme we will discuss in this chapter is the art of constant learning. Your greatest strengths in a financial environment that is changing quickly are your capacity to adapt and your insatiable curiosity. We'll talk about how to stay knowledgeable, flexible, and able to adjust to new financial opportunities and difficulties.

As you go through this chapter more, you'll see that financial literacy is a tool for achieving a goal that is a life of opportunity, abundance, and financial stability rather than an end in and of itself. In the pages that follow, you'll find expert viewpoints, useful advice, and doable actions to help you reach financial mastery. It's time to take the first step towards financial literacy and realize the full potential of your riches.

The Importance of Financial Literacy

The basis of financial empowerment is financial literacy. People can make wise financial judgments because they are equipped with the necessary knowledge. Financial literacy is becoming more and more important in this day and age of intricate financial instruments and a dynamic economy.

Understanding interest rates and navigating the complexities of investment options are just two examples of the many topics that fall under the umbrella of financial literacy. It involves knowing how to read and analyze financial statements, understanding the language of finance, and appreciating how different financial decisions affect one's long-term financial security.

Why is Financial Literacy Important?

1.   Knowledgeable   Decision-Making: Possessing financial literacy enables you to make knowledgeable financial decisions. This covers everything, from selecting the ideal loan or credit card to making prudent investing decisions.

2. Budgeting and Saving: The secret to efficiently developing and overseeing a budget is financial literacy. It teaches you how to plan for your financial objectives, save money, and track where your money is going.

3. Investing: You can confidently traverse the world of investments if you possess financial literacy. Since you are more aware of the possible outcomes and associated risks, you are in a better position to make decisions that support your financial objectives.

4. Responsible debt management is facilitated by financial literacy. You'll be aware of ways to lower your debt burden, comprehend the effects of various loan kinds, and steer clear of typical dangers.

5. Economic Security: Attaining economic security is the ultimate goal of financial literacy. It guarantees you have enough money

to maintain your intended lifestyle and acts as a safety net against unforeseen financial emergencies.

There are several methods available to improve your financial literacy, including Internet tools, financial advisors, books, and courses. Gaining financial literacy is an investment in oneself that will benefit you for the rest of your life.

Formal and Self-Education Roles

Education serves as the cornerstone for financial literacy. Learning about finance can be accomplished through two main methods: self-study and formal instruction.

Formal Education

Usually, formal education is provided in an organized setting, such as a school or university. Courses in business, finance, economics, and allied subjects are included. These courses offer a solid theoretical basis that is frequently supported by the most recent findings and industry insights. The following are some major benefits of formal education:

• Structured Learning: By adhering to a curriculum, formal education offers a planned route to financial literacy.

• Professional Advice: You can ask knowledgeable educators questions and receive professional advice.

• Credibility: In the employment market, formal degrees and certifications are respected as indicators of competence.

But formal schooling can be expensive and time-consuming, so it might not be an option for everyone. It's a good choice for anyone who wants to learn a lot about finance or is thinking about going into the industry.

Self-Education

Conversely, self-education provides accessibility and flexibility. It's self-directed learning, frequently motivated by needs and personal interests. Self-education resources abound and comprise the following:

• Books: An extensive collection of books on investment, personal finance, and related subjects.

• Online Courses: Renowned colleges and institutes provide a variety of financial courses through websites such as Coursera and edX.

• Websites and Blogs: A plethora of websites and blogs offer excellent, free financial guidance and information.

• Webinars and workshops: These online gatherings provide access to professional advice and the ability to speak with educators.

• Financial Advisors: Depending on your particular financial circumstances, working with a financial advisor might offer tailored advice.

Anyone can learn on their own, regardless of financial situation or background. It enables you to concentrate on the particular aspects of money that are most important to your objectives and way of life.

Creating a Robust Personal Finance Foundation

Before you can handle intricate financial planning or investing methods, you need to have a solid foundation in personal finance. This foundation gives your financial growth stability and nourishment, much like a tree's roots do.

The Elements of a Robust Personal Finance Base:

1. Budgeting: The foundation of personal finance is an efficient budget. It entails figuring out how much money you make and how much you spend to meet your demands and reach your financial objectives.

2. Saving: Saving is the process of reserving a part of your earnings for later usage. It's a crucial component of growth and financial security.

3. Emergency Fund: An emergency fund is a savings cushion designed to pay for unforeseen costs like auto or medical repairs. It keeps you out of debt if something unexpected happens in life.

4. Debt Management: It's important to comprehend the many forms of debt, their terms, and the most effective ways to pay them off. You may reduce your financial stress and save money by practicing good debt management.

5. Insurance: An insurance policy serves as a safety net to shield you from large financial losses. Health, vehicle, house, and life insurance are all included in this.

6. Making Retirement Plans: One of the most important aspects of personal finance is retirement planning. This entails knowing about retirement accounts, such as IRAs and 401(k)s, and calculating the amount you will require to live comfortably in retirement.

Establishing a solid foundation in personal finance paves the way for more sophisticated investing and financial plans. It's about planning for the future while safeguarding the present.

The Skill of Lifelong Learning

Learning financial literacy is a lifelong process rather than a single event. Understanding how constantly changing the financial world is is the art of continuous learning. What was effective yesterday might not be so tomorrow. You have to embrace lifelong learning if you want to succeed in this fast-paced world.

Advantages of Lifelong Learning

1. Adaptation: The financial landscape is ever-evolving. Regularly emerging are new tax legislation, economic trends, and investment opportunities. You can adjust to these changes by continuing to learn new things.

2. Optimisation: You can continuously improve your tactics as you get more knowledge about personal money. Better financial decisions, more effective tax planning, and increased investment returns can result from this.

3. Risk Management: Your ability to evaluate and control risks improves with increased knowledge of financial products and markets.

4. Innovation: You may take advantage of the newest instruments for financial management by staying up to date on financial innovations and technology through continuous learning.

5. Financial Independence: You may always be in charge of your financial future if you pursue lifelong learning. Instead of depending on the opinions of others, it gives you the ability to make wise decisions.

Take into consideration the following methods to embrace continuous learning:

• Go over articles and books: Read financial publications often to keep up with the newest concepts and trends.

Participate in seminars and workshops: Attend seminars and workshops where professionals discuss best practices and perspectives.

• Make Use of Technology: Make use of financial tools and applications to improve your money management.

• Seek Advice: When in doubt, don't be afraid to speak with financial experts.

Keep in mind that learning about finance is an investment in your future. The more knowledge you have, the more equipped you are to safeguard your financial security and realize your objectives.

In summary

Chapter 2, titled "Financial Education," has established the foundation for your financial empowerment path. We have discussed the value of establishing a solid foundation in personal finance, the role that formal and self-education play, the significance of financial literacy, and the skill of lifelong learning. Equipped with this awareness

Chapter 3: Budgeting and Saving

In your quest for financial prosperity, one of the most potent tools at your disposal is the art of budgeting and saving. This chapter, "Budgeting and Saving," is your gateway to understanding the essential practices that can help you take control of your financial life, reduce stress, and pave the way for wealth accumulation.

Let's begin by acknowledging that budgeting and saving are not merely financial disciplines; they are life skills. These practices are the foundation upon which your financial fortress will be constructed. In this chapter, we'll explore four vital components:

Imagine your financial life as a grand tapestry. It's woven together with threads of income and expenses, savings and investments, hopes, and dreams. The artistry of this tapestry hinges on your ability to master the delicate dance between two pivotal elements: budgeting and saving. This chapter, "Budgeting and Saving," opens the door to an understanding of these crucial aspects of financial success.

Budgeting is the meticulous art of financial planning. It is the process of understanding your income, calculating your expenses, and orchestrating a harmonious balance between the two. A well-constructed budget serves as a roadmap, guiding you toward your financial goals.

Within the pages that follow, we will not only discuss how to create a realistic budget but also delve into the psychological and practical aspects of budgeting. You will uncover the transformative power of taking control of your finances, rather than letting them control you.

Cutting unnecessary expenses is another fundamental element of budgeting. It involves making conscious choices about how you spend your money. By identifying and eliminating frivolous expenditures, you free up resources to bolster your financial future. We will explore various strategies to help you cut through the clutter, distinguish between wants and needs, and maximize the efficiency of your budget.

Automating your savings is a powerful technique that capitalizes on the advantages of modern technology. It ensures that a portion of your income is routinely set aside, promoting a disciplined approach to saving. We'll discuss how automation simplifies the process and why it's an invaluable habit for accumulating wealth.

As you continue your journey through this chapter, we will also uncover a financial secret – the magic of compound interest. This enchanting force is like a multiplier for your savings and investments, and it has the potential to turn small, consistent efforts into substantial wealth over time. We'll explore how compound interest works, where it can be harnessed, and how you can use it to your advantage.

But before we explore the intricacies of these topics, it's essential to grasp that budgeting and saving are not restrictive practices; they are instruments of financial liberation. By mastering the art of balancing your income and expenses, trimming the excess, and harnessing the power of compound interest, you are setting yourself on a path toward financial freedom and fulfillment. Let's embark on this enlightening journey of budgeting and saving, and unlock the potential to shape your financial future.

The foundations of sound financial management and expansion are saving and budgeting. Well-crafted budgets work as a financial road map and wise savings strategies supply the funds required to reach your long-term financial objectives. This chapter will cover the nuances of setting up a realistic budget, putting methods into place to reduce wasteful spending, automating savings, and taking advantage of compound interest. You will take charge of your financial future and create the foundation for long-term prosperity and financial stability by learning these vital skills.

ESTABLISHING A REASONABLE BUDGET

Recognizing Your Revenue and Outlays

It is essential to have a thorough awareness of your sources of income and expenses before beginning any budgeting process. A realistic evaluation of your income streams is made possible by identifying all of your sources of income, including investments, secondary sources of income, and primary earnings. You can see exactly where your money is going by keeping track of and classifying your expenses, including debt payments, discretionary spending, and necessities.

Establishing Priorities and Financial Goals

Making a realistic budget involves more than simply handling your present debts; it also entails future planning. Prioritizing your budgeting efforts is aided by setting attainable financial goals, such as saving for a certain milestone, paying off debt, or creating an emergency fund. When your budget is in line with your goals, both short- and long-term, each dollar you spend will have a specific use and will contribute to your overall financial health.

Developing a Financial Strategy

The creation of an extensive budget requires careful financial planning and distribution. This entails dividing expenditures into fixed and variable costs, setting up an emergency fund, and accounting for savings for retirement or future investments. The ultimate goal of an efficient budgeting plan is to balance your income and expenses in a way that permits both financial security and the pursuit of your financial goals.

Techniques for Staying Within Your Budget

To ensure that your budgeting strategy is implemented successfully, you must continue to practice financial discipline. You may stay on track and prevent needless financial detours by putting tactics like routine expense tracking, modifying spending habits to fit your goals, and routinely assessing and readjusting your budget into practice. Furthermore, taking a proactive stance while handling possible budgetary difficulties might support you in overcoming unforeseen financial obstacles with tenacity and resolve.

TECHNIQUES FOR REDUCING NEEDLESS EXPENSES

Differentiating Needs from Wants

Being able to differentiate between necessities and wants is one of the most important aspects of good budget management. You can find areas where you can decrease costs without sacrificing your overall quality of life by critically analyzing your spending patterns and setting priorities for important needs. Reducing needless expenditures can be greatly aided by adopting a mindset that promotes deliberate and thoughtful spending.

Putting Cost-Reduction Measures in Place

Using creative and proactive expense management is essential to implementing cost-cutting strategies within your budget. This can involve haggling over prices for bills and subscription services, looking into less expensive options for necessities, and taking advantage of sales or discounts for regular purchases. Through a proactive search for ways to cut costs without compromising on necessities, you may maximize your budget and direct more funds toward your financial objectives.

Developing Conscious Spending Practises

Creating a sustainable and ethical approach to money management requires you to cultivate conscious spending habits. This entails using self-awareness and self-control while making decisions about what to buy, abstaining from impulsive behavior, and placing worth and utility above fleeting pleasure. Your spending habits can be made healthier and more attentive by integrating mindfulness. This will reduce the likelihood of overspending and poor financial management.

SETTING UP AUTO-SAVINGS

How to Create an Emergency Fund

Establishing an emergency fund is essential to safeguarding your financial security and safeguarding against unanticipated financial emergencies. Regular contributions to your emergency fund can be automated to provide a safety net against unforeseen costs or interruptions in income. This will give you financial security and peace of mind. Setting aside a regular amount of money for emergencies strengthens your financial fortitude and equips you to face difficult financial situations head-on.

Making Use of Automated Transfers

One way to make sure you have regular and disciplined savings habits is to set up automatic transfers from your checking account to savings or investment accounts. You can simplify saving by automating transfers at pre-arranged periods, which also reduces the possibility that you will forget to make contributions to your savings during routine spending. This method encourages a methodical and structured approach to accumulating wealth, enabling you to proactively develop financial resources without having to deal with the hassles of manual savings management.

Increasing Retirement Benefits

One smart approach to safeguard your long-term financial security is to automate contributions to retirement accounts, such as individual retirement accounts (IRAs) or 401(k) plans. Employer-matched contributions and tax-deferred investing possibilities are two ways to start laying the groundwork for a safe retirement. Regularly setting aside a percentage of your salary for retirement helps you build wealth and develop confidence in your future financial prospects as well as a sense of financial readiness.

Compound Interest's Magic

Comprehending Compound Interest Concept

A strong financial concept called compound interest has the potential to greatly accelerate your attempts to build money over time. Your savings or investment portfolio will increase exponentially as a result of the reinvestment of previously earned interest. To take advantage of this phenomenon and increase the returns on your financial assets, it is essential to comprehend the principles of compound interest, principal amounts, interest rates, and compounding periods.

Taking Advantage of Compound Interest

Compound interest can only be fully realized by taking a long-term, proactive approach to wealth management. You can take advantage of the exponential growth potential of your financial assets by looking into investment possibilities that give compounded returns, such as retirement portfolios, mutual funds, or high-yield savings accounts. You may maximize the benefits of compound interest and build a strong, diversified financial portfolio by making well-informed, strategic investment decisions that are in line with your risk tolerance and financial goals.

Stressing the Importance of Consistency and Time

To fully utilize compound interest, two essential elements are time and consistency. The compounding effect on your overall financial progress increases with the length of time your investments stay untouched and earn interest. Making continuous and disciplined savings and investing a top priority helps you build a strong financial base that can weather market turbulence and take advantage of the gradual, steady increase made possible by compound interest. To fully benefit from compound interest, you must stress the importance of long-term financial planning and keep a strong commitment to your wealth-building goals.

In summary

Saving money and creating a budget are not only sound financial habits; they are also revolutionary lifestyle decisions that open doors to wealth and stability in the financial realm. You build the foundation for a sound and stable financial future by making a realistic budget, automating savings, reducing wasteful spending, and taking advantage of compound interest. Keep in mind that every financial choice you make today will help you achieve your long-term financial goals. Through the practice of budgeting and saving with awareness and initiative, you enable yourself to become financially independent and open the door to long-term riches and prosperity.

The foundations of sound financial management and expansion are saving and budgeting. Well-crafted budgets work as a financial road map and wise savings strategies supply the funds required to reach your long-term financial objectives. This chapter will cover the nuances of setting up a realistic budget, putting methods into place to reduce wasteful spending, automating savings, and taking advantage of compound interest. You will take charge of your financial future and create the foundation for long-term prosperity and financial stability by learning these vital skills.

ESTABLISHING A REASONABLE BUDGET

Recognizing Your Revenue and Outlays

It is essential to have a thorough awareness of your sources of income and expenses before beginning any budgeting process. A realistic evaluation of your income streams is made possible by identifying all of your sources of income, including investments, secondary sources of income, and primary earnings. You can see exactly where your money is going by keeping track of and classifying your expenses, including debt payments, discretionary spending, and necessities.

Establishing Priorities and Financial Goals

Making a realistic budget involves more than simply handling your present debts; it also entails future planning. Prioritizing your budgeting efforts is aided by setting attainable financial goals, such as saving for a certain milestone, paying off debt, or creating an emergency fund. When your budget is in line with your goals, both short- and long-term, each dollar you spend will have a specific use and will contribute to your overall financial health.

Developing a Financial Strategy

The creation of an extensive budget requires careful financial planning and distribution. This entails dividing expenditures into fixed and variable costs, setting up an emergency fund, and accounting for savings for retirement or future investments. The ultimate goal of an efficient budgeting plan is to balance your income and expenses in a way that permits both financial security and the pursuit of your financial goals.

Techniques for Staying Within Your Budget

To ensure that your budgeting strategy is implemented successfully, you must continue to practice financial discipline. You may stay on track and prevent needless financial detours by putting tactics like routine expense tracking, modifying spending habits to fit your goals, and routinely assessing and readjusting your budget into practice. Furthermore, taking a proactive stance while handling possible budgetary difficulties might support you in overcoming unforeseen financial obstacles with tenacity and resolve.

TECHNIQUES FOR REDUCING NEEDLESS EXPENSES

Differentiating Needs from Wants

Being able to differentiate between necessities and wants is one of the most important aspects of good budget management. You can find areas where you can decrease costs without sacrificing your overall quality of life by critically analyzing your spending patterns and setting priorities for important needs. Reducing needless expenditures can be greatly aided by adopting a mindset that promotes deliberate and thoughtful spending.

Putting Cost-Reduction Measures in Place

Using creative and proactive expense management is essential to implementing cost-cutting strategies within your budget. This can involve haggling over prices for bills and subscription services, looking into less expensive options for necessities, and taking advantage of sales or discounts for regular purchases. Through a proactive search for ways to cut costs without compromising on necessities, you may maximize your budget and direct more funds toward your financial objectives.

Developing Conscious Spending Practises

Creating a sustainable and ethical approach to money management requires you to cultivate conscious spending habits. This entails using self-awareness and self-control while making decisions about what to buy, abstaining from impulsive behavior, and placing worth and utility above fleeting pleasure. Your spending habits can be made healthier and more attentive by integrating mindfulness. This will reduce the likelihood of overspending and poor financial management.

SETTING UP AUTO-SAVINGS

How to Create an Emergency Fund

Establishing an emergency fund is essential to safeguarding your financial security and safeguarding against unanticipated financial emergencies. Regular contributions to your emergency fund can be automated to provide a safety net against unforeseen costs or interruptions in income. This will give you financial security and peace of mind. Setting aside a regular amount of money for emergencies strengthens your financial fortitude and equips you to face difficult financial situations head-on.

Making Use of Automated Transfers

One way to make sure you have regular and disciplined savings habits is to set up automatic transfers from your checking account to savings or investment accounts. You can simplify saving by automating transfers at pre-arranged periods, which also reduces the possibility that you will forget to make contributions to your savings during routine spending. This method encourages a methodical and structured approach to accumulating wealth, enabling you to proactively develop financial resources without having to deal with the hassles of manual savings management.

Increasing Retirement Benefits

One smart approach to safeguard your long-term financial security is to automate contributions to retirement accounts, such as individual retirement accounts (IRAs) or 401(k) plans. Employer-matched contributions and tax-deferred investing possibilities are two ways to start laying the groundwork for a safe retirement. Regularly setting aside a percentage of your salary for retirement helps you build wealth and develop confidence in your future financial prospects as well as a sense of financial readiness.

COMPOUND INTEREST'S MAGIC

Comprehending Compound Interest Concept

A strong financial concept called compound interest has the potential to greatly accelerate your attempts to build money over time. Your savings or investment portfolio will increase exponentially as a result of the reinvestment of previously earned interest. To take advantage of this phenomenon and increase the returns on your financial assets, it is essential to comprehend the principles of compound interest, principal amounts, interest rates, and compounding periods.

Taking Advantage of Compound Interest

Compound interest can only be fully realized by taking a long-term, proactive approach to wealth management. You can take advantage of the exponential growth potential of your financial assets by looking into investment possibilities that give compounded returns, such as retirement portfolios, mutual funds, or high-yield savings accounts. You may maximize the benefits of compound interest and build a strong, diversified financial portfolio by making well-informed, strategic investment decisions that are in line with your risk tolerance and financial goals.

Stressing the Importance of Consistency and Time

To fully utilize compound interest, two essential elements are time and consistency. The compounding effect on your overall financial progress increases with the length of time your investments stay untouched and earn interest. Making continuous and disciplined savings and investing a top priority helps you build a strong financial base that can weather market turbulence and take advantage of the gradual, steady increase made possible by compound interest. To fully benefit from compound interest, you must stress the importance of long-term financial planning and keep a strong commitment to your wealth-building goals.

In summary

Saving money and creating a budget are not only sound financial habits; they are also revolutionary lifestyle decisions that open doors to wealth and stability in the financial realm. You build the foundation for a sound and stable financial future by making a realistic budget, automating savings, reducing wasteful spending, and taking advantage of compound interest. Keep in mind that every financial choice you make today will help you achieve your long-term financial goals. Through the practice of budgeting and saving with awareness and initiative, you enable yourself to become financially independent and open the door to long-term riches and prosperity.

Chapter 4: Investing Wisely

Introduction: Planting the Seeds of Wealth

The skill of investing is comparable to sowing seeds with an eye toward future harvests on the path to financial success. Making intelligent investments involves more than just seeing your money grow; it also involves protecting it, tending to it, and making sure it blossoms into a veritable garden of riches. This chapter takes us on an exploration of the terrain of investment wisdom, revealing the keys to wise financial decision-making.

Allocating resources to generate returns in the future is the essence of investing. But this straightforward notion hides a complicated and varied world. This chapter will walk you through the fundamentals of investing, including risk management and diversification, as well as how to examine different investment vehicles, distinguish between long-term and short-term investing, and create a well-defined investment plan.

Managing Risk and Diversifying

The art of diversification involves distributing your investments across a range of assets to reduce risk. It's similar to spreading your investments across multiple accounts. In addition to raising your chances of making money, diversification lessens the negative effects of a single investment's underperformance on your portfolio as a whole. The concepts of risk management and diversification will be covered in detail in this section, which will help you make wise investment decisions that will protect your financial future.

Various Investment Vehicles: Real Estate, Bonds, Stocks, and More

There are many different routes in investing, and each has its particular topography. Knowing the features and possibilities of different investment vehicles is crucial, whether you're negotiating the wild world of stocks, the secure plains of bonds, or the concrete world of real estate. We'll give you an understanding of these various environments in this section so you can decide wisely where to spend your money.

Short-term versus long-term Investments

In the world of investments, time is a crucial element. Investing with a long-term or short-term view might have a big influence on your financial path. While short-term investments have the potential for rapid rewards, long-term investments frequently deliver steady, compound growth. They do, however, also carry a higher danger. We'll look at the subtleties of time in investing in this section so you can make an informed decision about whether to sow the seeds of riches for the future or go for faster rewards now.

Formulating a Financial Plan

Investing is a strategic discipline, not a random endeavor. Developing a clear investing strategy is similar to planning your financial itinerary. Reaching your financial objectives entails establishing specific goals, evaluating your risk tolerance, and choosing the appropriate asset mix. We will walk you through the process of creating a solid investing plan so that you can start investing with a plan and direction.

You will learn in this chapter that investing is about more than just numbers and markets; it's about comprehending the ideas that propel economic expansion. It's about taking good care of your financial garden and seeing it grow. You'll arm yourself with the information and resources necessary to make wise financial decisions as we delve into the realm of investment wisdom. Your financial future is planted by your choices, and if you make sensible choices, you will reap the benefits of prosperity, security, and wealth.

One of the most important steps on the road to financial success is investing, which is the skill of gradually increasing your wealth. However investing is a strategic discipline that requires careful planning, risk management, and knowledge of many investment possibilities. It's not just about buying stocks or following hot ideas. We will examine the fundamentals of prudent investing in this chapter, "Investing Wisely," which includes risk management and diversification, various investment vehicles, the differences between long-term and short-term investing, and the creation of a strong investment plan.

Managing Risk and Diversifying

One of the most effective strategies for reducing risk and increasing the likelihood of steady returns is diversification. The proverb that goes, "Don't put all your eggs in one basket," applies to the investment industry. Investing in a variety of assets, including stocks, bonds, real estate, and other investment possibilities, is known as diversification. By doing this, you lower the possibility that one investment may underperform and cause a big loss. As the foundation of wise risk management, diversification serves as your armor against the volatility of the financial markets.

The art of risk management and diversification will be covered in detail in this section. You'll discover how to put together a well-balanced portfolio that fits your risk tolerance and financial objectives. We'll delve into the nuances of asset allocation, assisting you in realizing the significance of a diverse investing portfolio to get a pleasing ratio of risk to return.

Various Investment Vehicles: Real Estate, Bonds, Stocks, and More

The world of investing is diverse and expansive, providing a multitude of choices for how to allocate your funds. Every investment instrument has unique features, possible rewards, and risk levels. For instance, stocks have a higher degree of volatility but also reflect ownership in a firm and have the potential for large gains. As opposed to other debt products, bonds are noted for their consistency and timely interest payments. Investments in real estate involve physical assets and have the potential to increase in value both capitally and rental revenue.

Your guide to comprehending the differences between these investment vehicles and more can be found in this section. We'll go over the benefits and drawbacks of each, enabling you to decide where to put your money on your risk tolerance and financial goals. By investigating these varied environments, you'll be more capable of selecting investments that support your objectives.

Investing: Long-term versus Short-term

When making financial decisions, time is a crucial component. Deciding to invest for the long term against the short term will have a significant effect on your financial path. Investments with a long time horizon—several years or longer—have the potential to develop steadily and multiply. They are appropriate for people who are ready to weather market swings and have a patient mindset.

Short-term investments, on the other hand, are usually riskier and seek rapid returns. For people who can actively manage their investments and can handle market volatility, they might be a good fit. The subtleties of time in investing will be examined in this section to assist you in selecting the best strategy given your financial objectives and risk tolerance.

Formulating a Financial Plan

Investing is a journey with certain goals; it's not an aimless pursuit. Creating an investment strategy is like deciding on a route for your financial journey. Establishing clear objectives, determining your risk tolerance, and selecting the ideal asset mix are all part of your approach.

We'll walk you through the process of developing a solid investing strategy in this section. Whether your financial goals are for retirement, school, or something else entirely, you'll learn how to define precise, quantifiable financial objectives. We'll talk about how crucial it is to recognize your risk tolerance and make investing decisions that are consistent with it. Your strategy is your financial road map; it will provide you with focus and direction as you make your way through the challenging world of investing.

You'll be well-equipped to create a sensible investment strategy if you can grasp the concepts of risk management, diversification, and comprehending various investment vehicles. You can also make well-informed selections regarding long-term versus short-term investing. This chapter will provide you with the tools to make wise investment decisions that will put you on the route to wealth, stability, and financial progress. It is your doorway into the world of investing knowledge. Together, let's investigate the world of prudent investing.

Chapter 5: Entrepreneurship and Income Generation

Entrepreneurship is a bright spot in the pursuit of wealth and financial independence. Driven by creativity, passion, and tenacity, it's not just a way to make money—rather, it's a way to take control of your financial future. "Entrepreneurship and Income Generation," Chapter 5, provides an overview of the world of entrepreneurship and a guide to generating different sources of revenue.

Investigating Business Possibilities

Being an entrepreneur means seeing opportunities where others perceive hurdles, coming up with solutions when others run into issues, and transforming concepts into profitable ventures. This chapter serves as a guide for locating and grabbing business opportunities. We'll break down the entrepreneurial attitude, examine the ever-changing world of entrepreneurship, and teach you the tools you need to realize your dreams.

Finding Your Interest and Ability

Competence and enthusiasm are the two main factors that propel prosperous business owners. Making money isn't the only goal; you should also focus on developing your talents, doing what you enjoy, and adding value to other people. The foundation of entrepreneurship is knowing how to use your abilities and identifying your passion. We'll assist you in discovering your special talents, igniting your passion, and directing you towards a business venture that complements both your financial and personal goals in this part.

Developing Several Income Streams: Diversification is a key income-generating strategy that extends beyond investing. You may be financially exposed if you only have one source of income. We'll discuss the idea of generating several sources of income in this part. You'll discover how to create extra income streams through side ventures, investments, freelancing, and passive income. You'll raise your prospective income and improve your financial stability by adopting this strategy.

Entrepreneurship and Job Security in Balance

A crucial concern is striking a balance between traditional job security and entrepreneurship. The careful balance between the comforts of steady work and the pursuit of entrepreneurial goals is discussed in this section. We'll share our knowledge on how to successfully handle the shift from employee to business owner, keep your finances stable in the beginning, and travel the entrepreneurial path without endangering your long-term financial stability.

Being an entrepreneur is a way of life and a philosophy that goes beyond simply launching a company. It's about putting value creation, risk-taking, and passion pursuit ahead of your financial future. This chapter will teach you the craft of generating revenue and becoming an entrepreneur, giving you the tools to set out on a path to financial independence. You can uncover your entrepreneurial potential and pave the way to financial success by looking into business prospects, figuring out what your interests and abilities are, setting up numerous revenue streams, and striking a balance between work security and entrepreneurship. Greetings from the realm of money generating and entrepreneurship.

Within the dynamic field of financial empowerment, the field of entrepreneurship is a bright spot. It provides a route fueled by creativity, passion, and tenacity that allows you to not only make a living but also shape your financial future. This chapter, "Entrepreneurship and Income Generation," serves as both a guide for generating numerous sources of income and your portal to a world of entrepreneurial discovery.

Investigating Business Possibilities

The art of entrepreneurship is converting ideas into reality, converting obstacles into chances, and creating something exceptional from the ground up. Whether your goal is to launch a company, grow a side business, or pursue a career as a freelancer, entrepreneurship gives you the power to control how your finances are shaped.

We will act as your compass in this part, helping you to recognize and take advantage of business opportunities. Cultivating an entrepreneurial attitude is the first step. This entails encouraging an innovative and creative culture, accepting measured risk-taking, and finding opportunities where others see barriers. It's about seeing each obstacle as a springboard for achievement.

Taking those moments of inspiration and turning them into successful businesses is the essence of the entrepreneurial journey. We'll go over how to conduct market research, write a business plan, and assess the viability of your business ideas. By the time you finish reading this part, you'll be ready to take on the world of entrepreneurship with the drive and vision to make your goals come true.

Finding Your Interest and Ability

Making a living that utilizes your abilities and connects with your passions is the true meaning of entrepreneurship, not merely focusing on financial gain. It's the point where your personal interests and professional goals converge to create a rewarding and successful career. This section is meant to be your manual for discovering your skills and igniting your passions.

Successful entrepreneurs do so because of their passion. It stops feeling like work and becomes a labor of love when you are passionate about what you do. Your entrepreneurial career starts at the point where your interests, talents, and market demand converge. Whether your interests are in technology, the arts, or a particular sector of the economy, we will assist you in discovering your passions and developing a company plan that plays to them.

Determining your abilities is equally important. The instruments that turn your passion into a career are your skills. We'll explore methods for evaluating your skill set, pinpointing your advantages and potential development areas, and provide suggestions on how to keep getting better and broadening your skill set.

You'll be in a better position to choose a business endeavor that not only fits with your interests but also makes use of your experience if you have a clear idea of your passion and skills.

Generating Several Revenue Sources

A single source of income can put one's finances in jeopardy. Similar to diversification investments, diversifying income is a wise strategy to improve financial security. We'll discuss the idea of generating several sources of income in this part.

These revenue sources can be of several kinds. You can think about freelancing or launching a side business to capitalize on your special talents and interests and make extra money. Investing in stocks, bonds, real estate, or other financial instruments is an additional option. You can also make money while you sleep with passive income streams like affiliate marketing, royalties, and rental income.

This section will offer advice on how to choose which additional sources of income, given your interests, abilities, and resources, are most appropriate for you. It will also discuss the value of time management and how to successfully juggle the demands of several sources of income.

You can improve your earning potential and financial security by diversifying your sources of income. This strategy continues to produce income in other areas while protecting against financial downturns in one. A key component of long-term financial success is diversification, which is a tactic for enhancing financial resilience.

Entrepreneurship and Job Security in Balance

Deciding to become an entrepreneur can be exhilarating and intimidating since it frequently entails taking measured risks. The thought of following entrepreneurship while maintaining job stability appeals to a lot of people. This section discusses striking a careful balance between the security of steady work and the pursuit of entrepreneurial goals.

We'll go over the processes of going from working for someone else to starting your own business, offering advice on how to handle the initial financial uncertainty and possible setbacks. You can reduce financial risk and guarantee a consistent source of income as your firm takes off by continuing to work at your current employment as you embark on your entrepreneurial endeavors.

We'll also talk about how critical it is to preserve financial stability in the early phases of business. This entails setting up a safety net, controlling discretionary spending, and gaining insight into your precise financial requirements.

While becoming an entrepreneur can lead to enormous financial success and personal fulfillment, it's important to find a balance that fits with your long-term objectives and risk tolerance. You may maintain the financial stability you've established through traditional employment while pursuing an entrepreneurial career by using the advice in this section.

The entrepreneurial path leads to self-realization, creativity, and financial fulfillment in addition to being a way to make a living. You may unleash your entrepreneurial potential and start along the road to financial prosperity by looking into business prospects, figuring out what your passion and abilities are, setting up numerous revenue streams, and striking a balance between entrepreneurship and job security. Greetings from the realm of money generating and entrepreneurship. Here's where your journey starts.

Chapter 6: Debt Management

In personal finance, debt is a double-edged sword that can either help you achieve your financial goals or trap you in a never-ending cycle of debt. Your financial well-being can be greatly impacted by how you handle debt. This chapter, "Debt Management," takes you on an adventure to learn the subtle differences between good and bad debt, tactics for paying it off, how to negotiate reduced interest rates, and the significant psychological effects of debt and financial stress.

Understanding Good vs. Bad Debt

Essentially, debt is a tool for finance, a means to an aim. However, not all debt is made equal. There are two types of debt: good debt which can help you advance financially and bad debt which can trap you in a never-ending cycle of financial difficulties.

Good debt frequently consists of investments that have the potential to increase in value or produce income over time, such as home mortgages or student loans used to pay for college. In the end, these debts may increase your net worth.

On the other hand, bad debt usually consists of credit card bills or high-interest loans that have interest rates that can jeopardize your financial stability. This type of debt can impede your financial development and result in several problems, such as stress and diminished financial independence.

We'll break down the differences between good and bad debt in this section to help you decide which kinds of debt are worthwhile taking on and which are better to avoid. The foundation of good debt management is a thorough comprehension of this distinction.

Methods for Reducing Debt

Many people set out on the journey of debt repayment in the hopes of being financially free. The several approaches to managing and getting rid of debt are covered in this section.

We'll explore tried-and-true strategies for creating a debt payback schedule, such as the avalanche and snowball systems, which offer organized ways to pay off several loans.

We'll also talk about how crucial it is to make a budget to set aside funds for debt repayment. This gives you a road map for methodically paying off your debt in addition to assisting you in prioritizing debt eradication.

In addition to paying your bills on time, managing your debt also entails communicating with creditors, looking into consolidation alternatives, and being aware of any potential effects on your credit score. You will have a toolbox full of techniques to efficiently pay off your debts by the end of this part.

Negotiating Lower Interest Rates

An important factor in the cost of debt is interest rates. Lower interest rates make repayment more reasonable, whereas higher rates can dramatically increase your debt load. We'll look at the art of negotiating reduced interest rates with creditors in this part.

We'll provide you with tips on how to contact creditors and present a strong argument for lowering interest rates, as well as insights into the negotiation process. You'll discover how to combine high-interest debt into lower-rate loans through balance transfer options and other methods. You might be able to reduce your debt repayment costs by thousands of dollars by becoming an expert in interest rate negotiating.

The Psychological Effects of Stress and Debt in Finance

Debt is a psychological and emotional burden in addition to a financial one. Stress and debt have a psychological toll that might compromise your general health. We'll talk about the several ways that debt might affect your relationships and mental health in this section.

We'll cover coping mechanisms for the psychological effects of debt, such as getting advice from financial counselors, learning stress-reduction methods, and taking action to stop financial stress from happening again in the future.

Taking care of the emotional aspect of debt management entails more than just maths. You may take back control of your financial situation and start along the road to long-term financial freedom by comprehending the psychological effects of debt and mastering effective debt management techniques.

Debt management is a journey of resilience and self-discovery rather than just a financial transaction. You may take control of your finances by learning what constitutes good and bad debt, putting debt repayment plans into action, negotiating lower interest rates, and taking care of the psychological effects of debt. This chapter is your road map through the debt minefield, assisting you in negotiating the challenges of debt management and ultimately locating the path to financial freedom.

The Debt Conundrum

Debt, a financial double-edged sword, has the power to either fuel your dreams or shackle you to a cycle of financial stress. How you manage your debt can significantly influence your financial future. In this chapter, "Debt Management," we'll explore the vital distinctions between good and bad debt, unveil practical strategies for conquering your debt, navigate the world of negotiating lower interest rates, and examine the profound psychological impact that debt and financial stress can have on your life.

Understanding Good vs. Bad Debt

Debt is a financial tool, but not all debt is created equal. There's good debt, which can be a strategic stepping stone toward financial growth, and then there's bad debt, which can drag you into a never-ending financial quagmire.

Good debt often involves investments that have the potential to appreciate or generate income over time. This could include a mortgage for a home, which not only provides shelter but also builds equity, or student loans that fund education, ultimately increasing your earning potential. Good debt, when managed wisely, can be an ally on your financial journey.

Bad debt, on the other hand, typically encompasses high-interest loans, credit card balances, and other debt that accumulates interest at rates that can erode your financial stability. It's the kind of debt that can keep you up at night, hinder your financial progress, and lead to a range of issues, from high-stress levels to diminished financial freedom.

This section will help you navigate the fine line between good and bad debt. By the end of it, you'll have a solid understanding of which debts are worth taking on and which are best left avoided, providing you with a strong foundation for managing your debt wisely.

Strategies for Paying Off Debt

The journey to debt freedom is one that many embark on with the hope of achieving financial liberation. This section will guide you through various strategies for managing and ultimately eliminating your debt.

We'll explore techniques for setting up a debt repayment plan, including popular methods like the snowball and avalanche approaches, which provide structured ways to tackle multiple debts. We'll also delve into the significance of creating a budget to allocate resources toward debt repayment. This not only helps prioritize debt elimination but also offers a structured approach to clearing your financial obligations systematically.

Effective debt management extends beyond just making payments; it's also about negotiating with creditors, exploring consolidation options, and understanding the potential impact on your credit score. By the end of this section, you'll be well-equipped with a toolkit of strategies to effectively pay down your debts.

Chapter 7: Building Wealth through Real Estate

Real estate, often called "bricks and mortar," has long been regarded as one of the most enduring and potentially lucrative investments. It offers numerous avenues to build wealth, from rental properties and property flipping to Real Estate Investment Trusts (REITs). In this chapter, "Building Wealth through Real Estate," we will explore these opportunities, providing insights into effective real estate investment strategies and the essential aspects of managing and maintaining real estate investments.

INVESTING IN RENTAL PROPERTIES

The Resilience of Rental Properties

Rental properties have an enduring appeal in the realm of real estate investment. Owning rental properties can provide a consistent stream of income, the potential for long-term capital appreciation, and a degree of control over your investment.

This section will guide you through the ins and outs of investing in rental properties. We'll explore:

Property Selection: The art of choosing the right property is critical. You'll learn about various property types, such as residential, commercial, and vacation rentals, and how to assess their income potential.

Financing Options: Real estate often requires substantial upfront investment. We'll discuss financing options, from traditional mortgages to creative financing strategies.

Property Management: Effectively managing a rental property involves finding and retaining tenants, maintaining the property, and ensuring compliance with legal and regulatory requirements. We'll provide tips for success in this area.

Calculating Returns: Real estate investment involves not only rental income but also the potential for property appreciation. We'll guide you through the process of calculating returns on your investment, including metrics like cash-on-cash return and the cap rate.

Risks and Rewards: As with any investment, real estate has its risks. We'll explore the potential challenges and rewards of rental property investment.

By the end of this section, you'll have a comprehensive understanding of how to invest in rental properties effectively, from property selection to ongoing management.

FLIPPING PROPERTIES FOR PROFIT

The Art of Property Flipping

Property flipping is an investment strategy that involves purchasing a property with the goal of renovating or improving it and then selling it for a profit. This approach offers the potential for significant short-term gains but also comes with higher risks.

In this section, we'll delve into the world of property flipping, providing insights into:

Property Selection: The first step in property flipping is choosing the right property. We'll discuss how to identify properties with profit potential and evaluate renovation costs.

Renovation and Improvement: Successful property flipping often hinges on effective renovation and improvement. You'll learn about the types of renovations that can add value to a property and how to manage the renovation process.

Financing and Budgeting: Property flipping typically requires short-term financing and a well-defined budget. We'll explore financing options and budgeting techniques to ensure a profitable flip.

Market Trends: Understanding market trends is crucial in property flipping. We'll provide tips for staying informed about local real estate markets and identifying opportunities.

Managing Risks: Property flipping carries inherent risks, such as unexpected renovation costs or market fluctuations. We'll discuss risk management strategies to mitigate potential challenges.

By the end of this section, you'll be equipped with the knowledge and strategies needed to engage in property flipping successfully.

REAL ESTATE INVESTMENT TRUSTS (REITS)

Passive Real Estate Investment

Real Estate Investment Trusts, or **REITs**, offer a passive and diversified way to invest in real estate. These investment vehicles pool funds from multiple investors to invest in various real estate properties, such as apartment complexes, office buildings, or shopping centers. They offer the potential for consistent income and a degree of diversification.

This section will provide an in-depth look at REITs, including:

Types of REITs: There are different types of REITs, including equity REITs, mortgage REITs, and hybrid REITs. We'll explore each type and discuss their unique characteristics.

Investment Process: Investing in REITs is straightforward. We'll guide you through the process of purchasing REIT shares, monitoring your investment, and receiving dividends.

Diversification Benefits: REITs offer a level of diversification that individual property ownership can't match. We'll explain how this diversification can reduce risk.

Tax Considerations: REITs have specific tax advantages and implications. We'll provide insights into the tax aspects of investing in REITs.

Risks and Rewards: Like any investment, REITs come with their own set of risks. We'll discuss the potential rewards and challenges of investing in REITs.

By the end of this section, you'll have a comprehensive understanding of REITs as an investment option and how to incorporate them into your portfolio effectively.

Managing and Maintaining Real Estate Investments

The Art of Effective Real Estate Management

Investing in real estate is just the beginning; effectively managing and maintaining these investments is crucial for long-term success. This section will cover the essential aspects of real estate management, including:

Tenant Management: If you own rental properties, managing tenants is a key responsibility. We'll discuss tenant selection, lease agreements, and strategies for maintaining positive landlord-tenant relationships.

Property Maintenance: Regular property maintenance is essential to preserve its value. We'll provide tips for keeping your real estate investments in top condition.

Legal and Regulatory Compliance: Real estate investments are subject to various laws and regulations. We'll discuss how to ensure your investments remain compliant and avoid potential legal issues.

Financial Management: Effective financial management is critical for real estate investments. We'll cover strategies for tracking income and expenses, budgeting for maintenance and renovations, and optimizing cash flow.

Long-Term Planning: Real estate investments are often part of a long-term financial strategy. We'll discuss how to incorporate these investments into your overall financial planning.

By the end of this section, you'll have the knowledge and tools necessary to manage and maintain your real estate investments effectively, whether they involve rental properties, property flipping, or REITs.

Conclusion

Real estate presents a world of opportunities for building wealth, from the stability of rental properties to the potential gains of property flipping and the diversification of REITs. However, successful real estate investment requires knowledge, careful planning, and effective management. This chapter has provided you with the foundational insights and strategies needed to navigate the world of real estate investment, opening the doors to the wealth-building potential it offers.

Chapter 8: Creating Passive Income

Many people aspire to financial independence, but getting there might present a number of difficulties. Throughout this trip, Chapter 8, "Creating Passive Income," provides guidance and insights into methods and opportunities for earning money without requiring regular hands-on work. The technique of assembling a portfolio of dividend-paying stocks, the realm of income production from royalties and intellectual property, the various passive income streams from investments and ventures, and the ultimate goal of achieving financial freedom are all covered in this chapter.

Building a Portfolio of Dividend-Paying Stocks

In the realm of investing, dividend-paying stocks are highly favoured. These stocks provide a consistent dividend income stream in addition to the possibility of capital growth. A thorough overview of the world of dividend investing is given in this section. We'll look at how to choose companies, how to create a diversified dividend portfolio, how effective dividend reinvestment is, and how dividend stocks can help you accumulate wealth over the long run. You'll have a firm understanding of how to take advantage of dividend-paying equities for passive income at the end of this section.

Making Money with Intellectual Property and Royalties

Intellectual property and royalties provide a special way to make passive income. The topic of intellectual property is covered in detail in this section, including books, music, patents, and more. We'll go over how to safeguard and profit from your intellectual property, the significance of licencing contracts, and the possibility of royalties as a steady source of revenue. You will be well-equipped to investigate the realm of intellectual property and royalties as a passive revenue stream at the end of this course.

Streams of Passive Income from Businesses and Investments

Innovative revenue streams and astute company endeavours can potentially yield passive income, in addition to conventional investments. This section provides a comprehensive overview of passive income, looking at peer-to-peer lending, real estate, internet ventures, and other innovative ways to make money with little daily effort. We'll explore the main ideas, dangers, and benefits connected to each of these sources of passive income. You will have a thorough understanding of the many, conventional and non-traditional paths to passive income by the end of this section.

Reaching Financial Independence

Financial independence is the journey's ultimate goal. This section is meant to be your roadmap to achieving this transformative objective. We'll talk about how to create specific financial goals, how to define financial freedom for yourself, and how to increase and sustain your passive income sources. You will gain knowledge on the significance of long-term investing, budgeting, and financial discipline. You'll have a road map for reaching the financial independence you've always desired by the time you finish this section.

This chapter serves as a doorway to a future in which you control money rather than it controlling you. In this environment, having financial freedom is a real possibility rather than just a pipe dream. Greetings from the realm of passive income creation, where achieving financial independence turns into an exciting path of empowerment, growth, and opportunity.

Chapter 9: Networking and Building Relationships

It is impossible to overestimate the importance of networking and forming relationships in the always changing world of wealth creation. "Networking and Building Relationships," Chapter 9, delves deeply into the priceless resources that connections and relationships can be on your path to financial success. This chapter will explore how to effectively use your network, the life-changing power of mentoring and coaching, the synergistic possibilities of cooperative partnerships for financial success, and the deeply meaningful effects of giving back to your community.

Making Use of Your Network's Power

Discovering the Secret Treasure of Relationships

Your network is a complex web of connections, both personal and professional, made up of individuals who may offer chances, wisdom, and assistance. This section will reveal your network's power and provide instructions on how to:

Grow Your Connections: We'll talk about how to expand your network using social media, professional associations, networking events, and community service.

Develop Partnerships: Creating real contacts is more important than just gathering business cards when building a strong network. We'll talk about the skill of creating and preserving partnerships based on mutual respect, trust, and gain.

Utilise Your Network: After you've built a strong network, it's time to make use of it. We'll talk about how to use your network to find opportunities, guidance, and assistance.

Offer Value: Building a network involves both parties. We'll stress how crucial it is to contribute to your network and serve as a resource for others.

By the time you finish reading this part, you will know how to use your network to its fullest financial potential.

Mentoring and advising

The Wisdom of Learning from Others

A strong catalyst for both financial and personal development is mentoring. It provides the chance to pick up knowledge from others who have already travelled the path you wish to take. We'll go into the world of mentoring in this part, offering insights into:

Locating a Guide: We'll talk about how to find possible mentors, whether they are in your current network or might be found through organisations and mentorship programmes.

Establishing a Mentorship Connection: The relationship between a mentor and mentee is distinct. We'll talk about the factors involved in creating and preserving a fruitful mentoring relationship.

Growth and Learning: A mentor can offer direction, expertise, and insight. We'll talk about how to get the most out of your mentorship and how it can help you improve.

Returning the Favour via Mentoring: Mentoring is a two-way relationship. We'll talk about the importance of giving back by taking on the role of mentor.

You will have a thorough knowledge of the role mentoring can play in your financial path and how to take full advantage of this life-changing relationship by the end of this section.

Collaborative Alliances for Economic Development

The Benefits of Collaboration

Financial growth is mostly driven by collaboration. In company or investing, partnerships can open doors that would be difficult to close on your own. This segment will investigate:

Finding Collaborative Opportunities: We'll talk about how to find possible collaborators and joint ventures that fit your budget.

Contracting and Forming Alliances: Gaining expertise in the art of partnership formation and negotiating is highly recommended. We'll offer advice on how to establish and preserve fruitful collaborations.

Distributing Rewards and Risks: As part of collaboration, profits and risks are frequently shared. We'll talk about how to handle these partnership management issues.

Collaboration as a means of diversification: Forming partnerships might help you diversify your business activities and investment portfolio. We will investigate the idea of diversification via cooperation.

By the time you finish reading this section, you'll know how to successfully traverse this dynamic domain and the potential benefits of collaborative partnerships for financial progress.

Contributing to Your Community

Community Engagement's Effects

Contributing to your community is not only a financial plan with long-term advantages but also a moral obligation. This section is going to explore:

Community Participation: We'll talk about the different ways you can give back to your community, like supporting small businesses and volunteering and donating to charities.

The Effect of Ripples Giving back has a significant effect on your financial and personal well-being in addition to your community. We'll look at how community involvement spreads.

The Community as an Asset: Another resource that can help you prosper financially is your community. We'll talk about ways to take advantage of the possibilities and assistance in your neighbourhood.

By the time you finish reading this part, you'll know how important it is to get involved in the community and how it can be a wise financial move.

This chapter serves as an entry point to a world of relationships, community involvement, mentoring, and teamwork. In this world, connections serve as inspiration, a catalyst for change, and more than simply a means to an end. Greetings from the world of relationships and networking, where your financial success is determined by the value of the connections you make.

Chapter 10: Tax Strategies

Taxes are an inevitable part of life, as they say, but they don't have to be a burden on your financial journey. In-depth discussion of tax efficiency is provided in Chapter 10, "Tax Strategies," which is an important but commonly overlooked aspect of building wealth. The complexities of the tax system, legal ways to lower your tax liability, the operation of tax-advantaged accounts, and the importance of seeking professional advice are all covered in this chapter.

Understand How the Tax Code Operates

The tax code is similar to a maze because of its many rules, credits, deductions, and restrictions. This section breaks down the tax code into digestible sections and demystifies it. You can use it as a guide. We'll examine:

• Tax Basics: An introduction to the fundamental concepts of taxes, including the many types of taxes and their effects on your own financial situation.

• Tax Credits and Deductions: A review of the various available credits and deductions, along with advice on how to make the most of them.

• Tax Planning: The ability to prepare ahead for taxes by choosing financially advantageous paths of action.

• Tax Filing: An overview of the tax filing process that include important deadlines and reminders.

By the time you complete this course, you'll have a solid understanding of the tax code and the foundation for creating a financial plan that minimises your exposure to taxes.

Legal Techniques to Lower Tax Obligation

It's not tax evasion that lowers your tax liability, but rather making prudent financial decisions that decrease your tax burden. This section will look at a few methods for achieving tax efficiency, such as:

• Tax-Efficient Investments: Methods for making intelligent financial decisions that reduce your tax liability.

The art of coordinating your income and deductions to maximise your tax benefits is known as the timing of income and deductions.

• Tax Planning for Different Life Stages: Strategies to reduce taxes at various life stages, from starting a career to retiring.

• Planning for Inheritance and Estate Taxes: Planning is essential for asset transfers in order to minimise tax implications.

By the time you finish this section, you will have the knowledge required to legally limit your tax liability and optimise your financial plan.

The Use of Tax-Advantaged Accounts

Tax-advantaged accounts can be useful tools for tax reduction. They offer opportunities for you to get richer and pay less in taxes. This section will look at the purpose of tax-advantaged accounts as well as:

• Retirement Accounts: The value of tax-advantaged retirement plans for future savings, such IRAs and 401(k)s.

• Health Savings Accounts (HSAs): Learn how these accounts can provide a triple tax benefit while reducing your medical costs.

• Education Savings Accounts: Methods for saving for college expenses through tax-advantaged accounts, such 529 plans.

• Tax-Advantaged Assets: The capacity to defer paying taxes on investments like municipal bonds and dividend equities.

By the time you finish this section, you will know more about the many tax-advantaged accounts that are accessible to you and how to incorporate them into your financial strategy.

Seeking Professional Advice

While knowing the principles of tax efficiency is important, navigating the ever-changing tax law landscape frequently requires professional assistance. In this section, we'll examine the role of tax professionals and discuss the following:

• Tax Advisors: The necessity of speaking with tax professionals, such as certified public accountants (CPAs) and tax attorneys.

• Financial Advisors: Their ability to provide thorough financial planning that considers tax efficiency.

• Tax Planning Services: Tax professionals offer these services, which range from long-term planning to tax preparation.

After reading this section, you will understand how important it is to get professional advice to ensure that your tax strategy aligns with your financial goals.

This chapter provides your road map to tax efficiency, which is a crucial part of building wealth. In this world, understanding the tax code, utilising tax-advantaged accounts, lowering your tax liability lawfully, and obtaining legal guidance are all essential to financial success. Greetings from the world of tax strategies, where becoming proficient in tax efficiency lets you keep more of your income and creates opportunities for a better financial future.

Section 10: Tax Planning

One essential aspect of our financial lives is paying taxes. They influence our economic environment and provide funding for infrastructure and vital public services. Nonetheless, it is essential for people to comprehend the tax code and use legal tactics to reduce their tax responsibility if they want to optimise their wealth and financial stability. We take a tour through the complex world of tax tactics in this chapter. We will explain the intricacies of the tax code, investigate legal ways to reduce your tax obligation, comprehend the function of tax-advantaged accounts, and stress the need of getting expert counsel.

KNOWING HOW THE TAX CODE WORKS

Understanding the Tax Maze

The tax law is an extensive collection of guidelines that control how people and companies file and pay their taxes. It may appear to be a maze of intricate clauses and legalese at first, but it is crucial to comprehend its basic elements. We'll demystify the tax code and give a basic overview of its important components in this part.

• Tax Fundamentals: An overview of the fundamentals of taxes, covering the many kinds of taxes and how they affect your financial situation.

• Credits and Deductions: An in-depth look at tax credits and deductions, crucial instruments for lowering your tax burden, and tactics for making the most of their application.

• Tax Planning: The skill of proactive tax planning, which entails weighing tax efficiency when making financial decisions.

• Tax Filing: A summary of the steps involved in filing taxes, along with crucial dates and factors to take into account in order to ensure accurate and timely filings.

You will have a thorough understanding of the fundamentals of the tax system by the end of this section, laying the groundwork for efficient tax planning.

Lawful Methods for Reducing Tax Obligation

Methodical Tax Cuts

Reducing your tax burden doesn't mean avoiding taxes; rather, it means using morally and legally sound methods to improve your financial circumstances. This section looks at some tax reduction techniques that can help you pay less in taxes while still abiding by the law.

• Tax-Efficient Investments: Strategies for minimising your tax obligation through well-informed investment decisions, such as capital gains optimisation and tax-efficient funds.

• Income and Deduction Timing: The skill of strategically arranging your income and deductions to optimise tax advantages, including year-end preparation.

• Life Stage Tax Planning: Techniques for minimising taxes at various phases of life, such as beginning a profession, preparing for retirement, and managing your assets after retirement.

• Estate and Inheritance Tax Planning: To reduce the tax impact on your assets and estate transfer, estate and inheritance tax planning is essential.

You will have the knowledge and skills necessary to use legal techniques to minimise your tax liability and maximise your financial plan by the end of this course.

Tax-Advantaged Accounts' Function

Taking Advantage of Tax-Advantaged Accounts' Power

An essential component of efficient tax planning and wealth building are tax-advantaged accounts. They provide chances to increase your wealth and reduce your tax burden. This section delves into the importance of tax-advantaged accounts and the ways in which they can facilitate your financial path.

• Retirement Accounts: Retirement accounts, like 401(k)s and IRAs, are essential for saving for the future while offering significant tax advantages.

• Health Savings Accounts (HSAs): HSAs offer a triple tax benefit that lowers your taxable income while allowing you to save for medical expenses.

• Education Savings Accounts: Ways to use 529 plans and other accounts to save tax-advantaged money for college costs, ensuring a better future for your loved ones.

• Tax-Advantaged Investments: Possibilities for tax efficiency improvement and wealth growth with investments like dividend equities and municipal bonds.

You will have a thorough understanding of the many tax-advantaged accounts available to you and how to incorporate them into your financial plan by the end of this part.

Getting Expert Guidance

The Benefits of Professional Advice

Keeping up with the ever-changing and complex world of tax regulations frequently calls for expert advice. This section will discuss the critical function that financial advisors and tax experts play in making sure that your tax plan is in line with your financial objectives.

• Tax Advisors: The need of consulting with tax experts, such as tax attorneys and certified public accountants (CPAs), and the range of services they offer, from long-term planning to tax preparation.

• Financial Advisors: These professionals provide comprehensive financial planning that takes tax efficiency into account and guarantees that your strategy is in line with your long-term goals.

• Tax Planning Services: The whole range of services provided by tax experts, such as ongoing tax planning, tax audits, and tax preparation.

By the time you finish this section, you will understand how crucial it is to consult a professional in order to successfully negotiate the tax planning difficulties and achieve tax efficiency in your overall financial plan.

This chapter is your guide to the complex world of tax tactics, where the cornerstones of financial success are knowing the tax code, legally reducing your tax liability, taking advantage of tax-advantaged accounts, and consulting a professional. Greetings from the world of tax efficiency, where you will discover how to save more of your earnings and build a strong foundation for a wealthy future.

Chapter 11: Overcoming Challenges and Staying on Course

Even though it is paved with goals and desires, the path to riches and financial success is frequently fraught with difficulties. Your journey's compass, Chapter 11, "Overcoming Challenges and Staying on Course," will lead you through any storms that may come. This chapter will cover how to overcome failures and setbacks, how to maintain motivation in the face of adversity, the adaptability of resilience, and the transformational potential of learning from mistakes.

Handling Failures and Setbacks

Failures and setbacks are unavoidable in life. These difficulties can show themselves in the field of wealth development as unanticipated financial crises, business setbacks, or investment losses. This section will provide details on:

• Resilience: One of the main characteristics of successful people is their capacity to overcome hardship. We'll look at techniques for growing resilient and courageously overcoming obstacles.

• Risk management: Effective risk management can lessen the effect of mistakes. We'll talk about the value of having a diverse portfolio and making backup plans.

• Mental Toughness: Overcoming obstacles requires developing your mental toughness. We'll offer advice on how to stay optimistic and build mental toughness.

By the time you finish reading this section, you will have the skills necessary to confront obstacles head-on and come out stronger on the other side.

Maintaining Motivation amid Adversity

The ability to stay motivated in the face of adversity is a quality shared by successful people. This section explores the skill of maintaining motivation in the face of adversity. We'll look at:

• Outlining Your Reason: Knowing your underlying driving forces can give you the strength to persevere in the face of difficulty. We'll talk about how important it is to define your "why."

• Goal Reevaluation: It's often essential to reevaluate your objectives and aspirations during difficult circumstances. We'll help you make the necessary adjustments to your goals while adhering to your long-term vision.

• Support and Mentoring: The inspiration and encouragement required to persevere can be obtained by asking peers and mentors for advice and assistance.

You'll have a better knowledge of how to maintain your motivation and drive in the face of big obstacles by the end of this part.

The Significance of Flexibility

In a world that is constantly evolving, flexibility is a crucial success factor. The need of adaptation in overcoming obstacles is emphasised in this section. We'll look at:

• Accepting Change: Life is full of change. We'll talk about how to embrace change and adjust to changing conditions.

• inventive Thinking: When overcoming obstacles, creative problem-solving and inventive thinking are crucial. We'll offer tactics for developing these abilities.

• Flexibility: Being adaptable in your financial tactics and goals will enable you to deal with unforeseen obstacles. We will discuss the significance of flexible financial planning.

By the time you finish reading this part, you will know how important it is to develop adaptability and the crucial role it plays in your financial path.

Taking Lessons from Errors

Even though they seem bad, mistakes teach us important things. This section explores the value of making errors and learning from them. We'll look at:

• Self-Reflection: One of the characteristics of successful people is their capacity to take stock of their activities and draw lessons from their errors. We'll offer techniques for productive introspection.

• Continuous progress: Developing wealth is a process that requires ongoing progress. We'll talk about how crucial it is to alter your financial tactics based on feedback.

• Risk Mitigation: Acknowledging mistakes entails developing plans to keep them from happening again. We'll look at risk reduction tactics and ways to steer clear of typical problems.

By the time you finish reading this part, you'll understand how learning from mistakes can change your life and be prepared to use setbacks as stepping stones to success in the future.

This chapter serves as a roadmap to help you through the inevitable obstacles you may face while pursuing your financial goals. It's a world in which failures are viewed as chances for improvement, inspiration drives your perseverance, flexibility is your strength, and errors are turned into insightful teaching moments. Greetings from the world of overcoming obstacles and keeping on course, where you can achieve financial success by tenacity, willpower, and the power of knowledge.

Chapter 12: Legacy and Giving Back

As we approach the last leg of our financial success trip, we delve into a dimension of wealth that goes beyond figures on balance sheets. In Chapter 12, "Legacy and Giving Back," the author explores the significance of the legacy one leaves behind, the practise of philanthropy and charitable giving, the intricate relationship between wealth and moral principles, and how to lead a happy and meaningful life that transcends material possessions.

Leaving Future Generations with a Financial Legacies

A person's ability to leave a lasting legacy for future generations, rather than just accumulating wealth during their lifetime, is a true indicator of their financial success. The idea of leaving a financial legacy for your heirs will be discussed in this part, along with methods for making sure your wealth has a beneficial effect even after you pass away. We'll explore:

• Wealth Transfer Planning: The skill of creating an all-inclusive strategy, including estate planning, trusts, and wills, for the transfer of assets to your loved ones.

• Financial Education: Educating the next generation about money matters and teaching strong financial ideals in order to prepare them for responsible wealth management.

• Philanthropic Legacy: How your generosity and philanthropy, such as the creation of charity trusts and family foundations, shape your legacy.

• Values and Ethics: The significance of leaving behind moral and ethical principles in addition to material possessions in order to leave a legacy that transcends time and space.

You will have a solid understanding of how to create a long-lasting financial legacy for your beneficiaries and successors by the time you finish this part.

Philanthropy and Charitable Giving: Possessing wealth gives one the ability to positively impact the lives of others. This section explores how your wealth may be a force for good by delving into the realm of philanthropy and charity giving. We'll explore:

• The Joy of Giving: The inherent benefits of generosity, such as the happiness and feeling of accomplishment that arise from contributing to worthy causes.

• Strategic Giving: The skill of strategic philanthropy entails choosing causes and organisations carefully so that they complement your objectives and ideals.

• Impactful Giving: Techniques for making the most of your philanthropic contributions, such as successful grant-making and impact investment.

• Legacy of Giving: The importance of leaving a philanthropic legacy that will survive for many generations and carry on supporting the causes you care about.

After reading this part, you will have the information and motivation necessary to start a journey of charitable giving and meaningful giving.

Wealth's Effect on Individual Values

Wealth frequently has a significant impact on an individual's personal values and views as it increases. This section examines the intricate relationship that exists between personal ideals and wealth, including:

• Self-Reflection: It's critical to regularly examine yourself in order to comprehend how your riches has shaped your priorities and values.

• Balancing Materialism: Techniques for keeping a sensible viewpoint and making sure that material prosperity doesn't eclipse life's most significant experiences.

• Personal Values and Decision-Making: Make sure your financial choices reflect your ethical convictions and personal values.

• Transmitting Values: The importance of passing on your basic principles to your descendants and fostering a family environment that upholds them.

You will have a better knowledge of how riches can affect your personal values and how to make sure they stay true to who you really are at the end of this part.

Living a Meaningful and Happy Life Despite Not Having Much Money

The capacity to live a happy and meaningful life is the ultimate goal of wealth, not just material success. In examining how to live beyond riches, this part focuses on the following: • Personal Fulfilment: Techniques for achieving contentment and personal fulfilment regardless of one's financial situation.

• Legacy of Wisdom: The value of enhancing the lives of others around you by imparting the knowledge you've acquired from your financial path.

• Meaningful Pursuits: Whether they are personal or professional endeavours, the pursuit of meaningful and purposeful activities that provide happiness and pleasure.

• Balanced Living: Reaching a state of peaceful equilibrium between material possessions and other facets of life, such relationships, health, and personal development.

You'll be ready to embrace a life of fulfilment and purpose that transcends material wealth by the time you finish this part.

This chapter serves as your road map to leaving a lasting legacy, the importance of giving back, how wealth affects personal values, and how to lead a meaningful life. In this world, having riches may be an instrument for good, and your legacy serves as a symbol of your moral character and the long-lasting difference you make in the world. Welcome to the world of legacy and giving back, where you can find the true meaning of wealth in the great changes you bring about in people's lives.